Laura Marsden

The Manipulation of Language in "Frankenstein"

Close analysis of Volume II, chapter IV

GRIN Publishing

Bibliographic information published by the German National Library:

The German National Library lists this publication in the National Bibliography; detailed bibliographic data are available on the Internet at http://dnb.dnb.de .

Imprint:

Copyright © 2014 GRIN Verlag GmbH
Print and binding: Books on Demand GmbH, Norderstedt Germany
ISBN: 978-3-656-87266-5

This book at GRIN:

http://www.grin.com/en/e-book/286923/the-manipulation-of-language-in-franken-stein

GRIN - Your knowledge has value

Since its foundation in 1998, GRIN has specialized in publishing academic texts by students, college teachers and other academics as e-book and printed book. The website www.grin.com is an ideal platform for presenting term papers, final papers, scientific essays, dissertations and specialist books.

Visit us on the internet:

http://www.grin.com/

http://www.facebook.com/grincom

http://www.twitter.com/grin_com

Frankenstein's creature attempts to integrate himself into society numerous times before he accepts that his physical defects and 'ugly' aesthetic appearance arouse fear in humanity; this separation from humanity forces him to discover alternative modes of integration. He "long[s]" to be part of civilisation yet he has been conditioned to recognise his dissemblance through victimisation.[1] Therefore he "dares not" present himself to the cottagers, vowing to "discover the motives" behind individual relationships.[2] In this essay I will argue that the Monster instinctively discovers the importance of language as well as the ability to manipulate language as a means of gaining companionship.

The purpose of the Monster's narrative in this passage is to emotionally provoke Frankenstein so he consents to create another being as "horrible" as the Monster himself.[3] Peter Brooks argues:

From his initial experience of language, the monster intuitively grasps that it will be important to him because by its very nature it implies the "chain of existence and events" within which he seeks a place defines the interdependency of senders and receivers of messages in that chain, and provides the possibility of emotional effect...[4]

In other words, it is language that holds the possibility of human interaction and thus human companionship. What the Monster observes and what Brooks suggests is that language relies on an 'interdependency' between individuals as one must 'receive' whilst the other 'sends'. This notion is physicalized in the passage. Initially the Monster can neither understand nor speak language and therefore exists separately from humanity. He is confined to the outdoor space whilst the cottagers are able to enjoy the comfort of one another inside. The outdoors which the Monster inhabits is bestialised as he "lay on [his] straw" in a "hovel"; traditionally associated with sheltering cattle.[5] The

[1] Mary Shelley, *Frankenstein* (Hertfordshire: Wordsworth Editions, 1993), p.85.

[2] Ibid., p.85.

[3] Ibid., p.111.

[4] Peter Brooks, 'Godlike Science/Unhallowed Arts: Language and Monstrosity in Frankenstein', *New Literary History*, Vol. 9 (1978), pp.591-605 (p.594).

[5] Mary Shelley, *Frankenstein* (Hertfordshire: Wordsworth Editions, 1993), p.85.

animal imagery that the monster adopts when relating his narrative demonstrates his self-classification as a "being" separate from humanity.[6] Conversely, the family's cottage is associated with warmth, both physical as a result of the "fire" but also metaphorical due to the music played by the "old man...on his instrument."[7] The familial intimacy which derives from the "love and respect" the younger generation bestow upon their elderly companion heightens the sense of togetherness which the Monster is palpably distanced from.[8]The separation between humanity and the Monster is furthered in the passage by the use of subject pronouns. The first person narrative structure lends to the Monster's constant use of 'I' and consequently the cottagers are labelled 'The boy', 'The Girl', or 'They'; never does the Monster indulge in 'We' or 'Us' when discussing the cottagers.[9] The language therefore heightens the physical separation between the Monster and humanity. By learning the language he can eradicate the boundary that his aesthetic appearance has created.

Due to the Monster's retrospective narrative, he evidently learns language. However, the sophisticated and elevated style which the Monster employs demonstrates the art of manipulation. Shelley explores the concept of language as a form of manipulation throughout the novel, as Beth Newman observes; even "Walton suggests that Frankenstein's eloquence- his fluency with words and his ability to manipulate language" has a powerful effect on the crew.[10] The Monster seems to share this skill. The passage itself exists almost as two narratives, the first being a factual documentation where the monster relates events as they occurred: "The young man was constantly employed outdoors, and the girl in various laborious occupations within..."[11] And the second, a stylised literary text in which the Monster consciously marginalises himself in order to evoke a compassionate response from Frankenstein. This is identifiable through the excessive adjectives such as "delicious viands", "deeply affected" and "delightful house" which are interspersed within the factual report of

[6] Ibid., p.86

[7] Ibid., p.86/ Ibid., p.85.

[8] Ibid., p.85

[9] Ibid., p.85.

[10] Beth Newman, 'Narratives of seduction and the Seductions of Narrative: The frame structure of Frankenstein', *ELH*, Vol. 53 (1986), pp.141-163 (p.145).

[11] Mary Shelley, *Frankenstein* (Hertfordshire: Wordsworth Editions, 1993), p.85.

events.[12] The alliteration and the elongated sound that the 'de…' creates emphasises the adjective and therefore romanticises what the Monster lacks; deepening his misfortune and consequently augmenting the reader's sympathy. The use of rhetorical questions such as: "what did their tears imply? Did they really express pain?" further the notion that the Monster has created a cultivated piece of literature.[13] Rhetorical questions are a language technique most typically associated with persuasive writing and the fact they appear directly next to one another in the passage heighten their persuasive power. The Monster is thus aware of this sophisticated language technique and has employed it in order to persuade Frankenstein. Similarly, the Monster includes the eloquent technique of the aside: "they possessed a delightful house (for such it was in my eyes)."[14] The bracketed aside places the Monster's personal interjection as a separate entity from the narrative, subsequently causing it to become a focal point. For the Monster, what the aside achieves is an indulgent shift in focus from the cottagers to his personal misfortune. By romanticising the cottagers and belittling himself as an "imperfect and solitary being" the Monster is able to intensify his misfortune; manipulating language to consciously enhance his inferiority.[15]

However, whilst the Monster romanticises the cottagers he also subtly debases humanity in a wider context. As mentioned the Monster employs an animalistic lexical field in order to highlight his inadequacy, but it is the humans who hold the status of 'animals' in this extract. The Monster labels them as "barbarous", a term with the definition: "uncivilised, rude, rough, wild and savage".[16] In addition, the Monster refers to the cottagers as "creatures", a word which becomes interchangeable between man and beast throughout the novel.[17] Not only does this animalistic representation serve to

---

[12] Ibid., p.86.

[13] Ibid., p.86.

[14] Ibid., p.86.

[15] Ibid., p.86.

[16] "Barbarous, adj.", *OED Online* (Oxford University press, September 2014) <http://www.oed.com> [Accessed 14th November 2014].

[17] Mary Shelley, *Frankenstein* (Hertfordshire: Wordsworth Editions, 1993), p.86.

foreshadow destructive events that will occur between the Monster and the cottagers but it also heightens the sympathy evoked for the Monster as he presents himself to be the prey within a world of predators.

Frankenstein is a novel of embedded narratives. Whilst this passage is from the perspective of the Monster it sits beneath the narrative voice of both Frankenstein and Walton. Arguably the Monster's intentions to manipulate language have been successful as Frankenstein allows his audience to feel sympathy for the Monster. With the knowledge that the latter is a murderer, Frankenstein could present the Monster negatively, however he allows the Monster moments of sympathy in his narrative to Walton. For example, the Monster highlights his personal "suffer[ing]", which the OED defines as "the bearing or undergoing of pain and distress", thus if Frankenstein had not been moved and affected by the Monster's narrative, it is unlikely he would allow a sympathetic interpretation of the Monster's character.[18] One can therefore conclude that the Monster's intentions to learn and utilise language in order to gain companionship and evoke sympathy have been successful.

Bibliography

- Brooks, Peter, 'Godlike Science/Unhallowed Arts: Language and Monstrosity in Frankenstein', *New Literary History*, Vol. 9 (1978), pp.591-605

- Newman, Beth, 'Narratives of seduction and the Seductions of Narrative: The frame structure of Frankenstein', *ELH*, Vol. 53 (1986), pp.141-163 (p.145).

- *OED Online* (Oxford University press, September 2014) <http://www.oed.com> [Accessed 14th November 2014]

- Shelley, Mary, *Frankenstein* (Hertfordshire: Wordsworth Editions, 1993)

---

[18] Ibid., p.85./ "Suffering, n", *OED Online* (Oxford University press, September 2014) <http://www.oed.com> [Accessed 14th November 2014].